The Gospel of Mark

NEW INTERNATIONAL READER'S VERSION

Hodder & Stoughton

LONDON SYDNEY AUCKLAND

Mark

John the Baptist Prepares the Way

1 This is the beginning of the good news about Jesus Christ, the Son of God.

²Long ago Isaiah the prophet wrote,

"I will send my messenger ahead of you.
    He will prepare your way."

[MALACHI 3:1]

³"A messenger is calling out in the desert,
'Prepare the way for the Lord.
    Make straight paths for him.'"

[ISAIAH 40:3]

⁴And so John came. He baptised people in the desert. He also preached that people should be baptised and turn away from their sins. Then God would forgive them. ⁵All the people from the countryside of Judea went out to him. All the people from Jerusalem went too. When they admitted they had sinned, John baptised them in the River Jordan. ⁶John wore clothes made out of camel's hair. He had a leather belt round his waist. And he ate locusts and wild honey.

[7]Here is what John was preaching. "After me, one will come who is more powerful than I am. I'm not good enough to bend down and untie his sandals. [8]I baptise you with water. But he will baptise you with the Holy Spirit."

Jesus Is Baptised and Tempted

[9]At that time Jesus came from Nazareth in Galilee. John baptised him in the River Jordan. [10]Jesus was coming up out of the water. Just then he saw heaven being torn open. He saw the Holy Spirit coming down on him like a dove. [11]A voice spoke to him from heaven. It said, "You are my Son, and I love you. I am very pleased with you."

[12]At once the Holy Spirit sent Jesus out into the desert. [13]He was in the desert for 40 days. There Satan tempted him. The wild animals didn't harm Jesus. Angels took care of him.

Jesus Chooses the First Disciples

[14]After John was put in prison, Jesus went into Galilee. He preached God's good news. [15]"The time has come," he said. "The kingdom of God is near. Turn away from your sins and believe the good news!"

[16]One day Jesus was walking beside the Sea of Galilee. There he saw Simon and his brother Andrew. They were throwing a net into the lake. They were fishermen. [17]"Come. Follow me," Jesus said. "I will make you fishers of men."

[18]At once they left their nets and followed him.

[19]Then Jesus walked a little farther. As he did, he saw James, son of Zebedee, and his brother John. They were in a boat preparing their nets. [20]There and then he called out to them. They left their father Zebedee in the boat with the hired men. Then they followed Jesus.

Jesus Drives Out an Evil Spirit

²¹Jesus and those with him went to Capernaum. When the Sabbath day came, he went into the synagogue. There he began to teach. ²²The people were amazed at his teaching. He taught them as one who had authority. He did not talk as the teachers of the law.

²³Just then a man in their synagogue cried out. He was controlled by an evil spirit. He said, ²⁴"What do you want with us, Jesus of Nazareth? Have you come to destroy us? I know who you are. You are the Holy One of God!"

²⁵"Be quiet!" said Jesus firmly. "Come out of him!"

²⁶The evil spirit shook the man wildly. Then it came out of him with a scream.

²⁷All the people were amazed. So they asked each other, "What is this? A new teaching! And with so much authority! He even gives orders to evil spirits, and they obey him." ²⁸News about Jesus spread quickly all over Galilee.

Jesus Heals Many People

²⁹Jesus and those with him left the synagogue. At once they went with James and John to the home of Simon and Andrew. ³⁰Simon's mother-in-law was lying in bed. She had a fever. They told Jesus about her. ³¹So he went to her. He took her hand and helped her up. The fever left her. Then she began to serve them.

³²That evening after sunset, the people brought to Jesus all who were ill. They also brought all who were controlled by demons. ³³All the people in the town gathered at the door. ³⁴Jesus healed many of them. They had all kinds of illnesses. He also drove out many demons. But he would not let the demons speak, because they knew who he was.

Jesus Prays in a Quiet Place

³⁵It was very early in the morning and still dark. Jesus got up and left the house. He went to a place where he could be alone. There he prayed. ³⁶Simon and his friends went to look for Jesus. ³⁷When they found him, they called out, "Everyone is looking for you!"

³⁸Jesus replied, "Let's go somewhere else. I want to go to the nearby towns. I must preach there also. That is why I have come." ³⁹So he travelled all through Galilee. He preached in their synagogues. He also drove out demons.

Jesus Heals a Man Who Had a Skin Disease

⁴⁰A man who had a skin disease came to Jesus. On his knees he begged Jesus. He said, "If you are willing to make me 'clean', you can do it."

⁴¹Jesus was filled with deep concern. He reached out his hand and touched the man. "I am willing to do it," he said. "Be 'clean'!" ⁴²At once the disease left him. He was healed.

⁴³Jesus sent him away at once. He gave the man a strong warning. ⁴⁴"Don't tell this to anyone," he said. "Go and show yourself to the priest. Offer the sacrifices that Moses commanded. It will be a witness to the priest and the people that you are 'clean'."

⁴⁵But the man went out and started talking right away. He spread the news to everyone. So Jesus could no longer enter a town openly. He stayed outside in lonely places. But people still came to him from everywhere.

Jesus Heals a Man Who Could Not Walk

2 A few days later, Jesus entered Capernaum again. The people heard that he had come home. ²So many people gathered that there was no room left. There was not even room outside the door. And Jesus preached the word to them.

³Four of those who came were carrying a man who could not walk. ⁴But they could not get him close to Jesus because of the crowd. So they made a hole in the roof above Jesus. Then they lowered the man through it on a mat.

⁵Jesus saw their faith. So he said to the man, "Son, your sins are forgiven."

⁶Some teachers of the law were sitting there. They were thinking, ⁷"Why is this fellow talking like that? He's saying a very evil thing! Only God can forgive sins!"

⁸Jesus knew at once what they were thinking. So he said to them, "Why are you thinking these things? ⁹Is it easier to say to this man, 'Your sins are forgiven'? Or to say, 'Get up, take your mat and walk'? ¹⁰I want you to know that the Son of Man has authority on earth to forgive sins."

Then Jesus spoke to the man who could not walk. ¹¹"I tell you," he said, "get up. Take your mat and go home."

¹²The man got up and took his mat. Then he walked away while everyone watched. All the people were amazed. They praised God and said, "We have never seen anything like this!"

Jesus Chooses Levi

¹³Once again Jesus went out beside the Sea of Galilee. A large crowd came to him. He began to teach them. ¹⁴As he walked along he saw Levi, son of Alphaeus. Levi was sitting at the tax collector's booth. "Follow me," Jesus told him. Levi got up and followed him.

¹⁵Later Jesus was having dinner at Levi's house. Many tax collectors and "sinners" were eating with him and his disciples. They were part of the large crowd following Jesus.

¹⁶Some teachers of the law who were Pharisees were there. They saw Jesus eating with "sinners" and tax collectors. So

they asked his disciples, "Why does he eat with tax collectors and 'sinners'?"

¹⁷Jesus heard that. So he said to them, "Those who are healthy don't need a doctor. People who are ill do. I have not come to get those who think they are right with God to follow me. I have come to get sinners to follow me."

Jesus Is Asked About Fasting

¹⁸John's disciples and the Pharisees were going without eating. Some people came to Jesus. They said to him, "John's disciples are fasting. The disciples of the Pharisees are also fasting. But your disciples are not. Why aren't they?"

¹⁹Jesus answered, "How can the guests of the bridegroom go without eating while he is with them? They will not fast as long as he is with them. ²⁰But the time will come when the bridegroom will be taken away from them. On that day they will go without eating.

²¹"People don't sew a patch of new cloth on old clothes. If they do, the new piece will pull away from the old. That will make the tear worse. ²²People don't pour new wine into old wineskins. If they do, the wine will burst the skins. Then the wine and the wineskins will both be destroyed. No, everyone pours new wine into new wineskins."

Jesus Is Lord of the Sabbath Day

²³One Sabbath day Jesus was walking with his disciples through the cornfields. The disciples began to break off some heads of corn. ²⁴The Pharisees said to Jesus, "Look! It is against the law to do this on the Sabbath. Why are your disciples doing it?"

²⁵He answered, "Haven't you ever read about what David did? He and his men were hungry. They needed food. ²⁶It was

when Abiathar was high priest. David entered the house of God and ate the holy bread. Only priests were allowed to eat it. David also gave some to his men."

²⁷Then Jesus said to them, "The Sabbath day was made for man. Man was not made for the Sabbath day. ²⁸So the Son of Man is Lord even of the Sabbath day."

3 Another time Jesus went into the synagogue. A man with a weak and twisted hand was there. ²Some Pharisees were trying to find fault with Jesus. They watched him closely. They wanted to see if he would heal the man on the Sabbath day.

³Jesus spoke to the man with the weak and twisted hand. "Stand up in front of everyone," he said.

⁴Then Jesus asked them, "What does the Law say we should do on the Sabbath day? Should we do good? Or should we do evil? Should we save life? Or should we kill?" But no-one answered.

⁵Jesus looked round at them in anger. He was very upset because their hearts were stubborn. Then he said to the man, "Stretch out your hand." He stretched it out, and his hand was as good as new.

⁶Then the Pharisees went out and began to make plans with the Herodians. They wanted to kill Jesus.

Crowds Follow Jesus

⁷Jesus went off to the Sea of Galilee with his disciples. A large crowd from Galilee followed. ⁸People heard about all that Jesus was doing. And many came to him. They came from Judea, Jerusalem, and Idumea. They came from the lands east of the River Jordan. And they came from around Tyre and Sidon.

⁹Because of the crowd, Jesus told his disciples to get a small boat ready for him. This would keep the people from crowding

him. [10]Jesus had healed many people. So those who were ill were pushing forward to touch him.

[11]When people with evil spirits saw him, they fell down in front of him. The spirits shouted, "You are the Son of God." [12]But Jesus ordered them not to tell who he was.

Jesus Appoints the Twelve Apostles

[13]Jesus went up on a mountainside. He called for certain people to come to him, and they came. [14]He appointed 12 of them and called them apostles. From that time on they would be with him. He would also send them out to preach. [15]They would have authority to drive out demons.

[16]So Jesus appointed the Twelve. Simon was one of them. Jesus gave him the name Peter. [17]There were James, son of Zebedee, and his brother John. Jesus gave them the name Boanerges. Boanerges means Sons of Thunder. [18]There were also Andrew, Philip, Bartholomew, Matthew, Thomas, and James, son of Alphaeus. And there were Thaddaeus and Simon the Zealot. [19]Judas Iscariot was one of them too. He was the one who was later going to hand Jesus over to his enemies.

Jesus and Beelzebub

[20]Jesus entered a house. Again a crowd gathered. It was so large that Jesus and his disciples were not even able to eat. [21]His family heard about this. So they went to take charge of him. They said, "He is out of his mind."

[22]Some teachers of the law were there. They had come down from Jerusalem. They said, "He is controlled by Beelzebub! He is driving out demons by the power of the prince of demons."

[23]So Jesus called them over and spoke to them by using stories. He said, "How can Satan drive out Satan? [24]If a kingdom fights against itself, it can't stand. [25]If a family is divided,

it can't stand. [26]And if Satan fights against himself, and his helpers are divided, he can't stand. That is the end of him. [27]In fact, none of you can enter a strong man's house and just take away what the man owns. You must first tie him up. Then you can rob his house.

[28]"What I'm about to tell you is true. Everyone's sins and evil words against God will be forgiven. [29]But anyone who speaks evil things against the Holy Spirit will never be forgiven. His guilt will last for ever."

[30]Jesus said this because the teachers of the law were saying, "He has an evil spirit."

Jesus' Mother and Brothers

[31]Jesus' mother and brothers came and stood outside. They sent someone in to fetch him. [32]A crowd was sitting around Jesus. They told him, "Your mother and your brothers are outside. They are looking for you."

[33]"Who is my mother? Who are my brothers?" he asked.

[34]Then Jesus looked at the people sitting in a circle round him. He said, "Here is my mother! Here are my brothers! [35]Anyone who does what God wants is my brother or sister or mother."

The Story of the Farmer

4 Again Jesus began to teach by the Sea of Galilee. The crowd that gathered round him was very large. So he got into a boat. He sat down in it out on the lake. All the people were along the shore at the water's edge. [2]He taught them many things by using stories.

In his teaching he said, [3]"Listen! A farmer went out to plant his seed. [4]He scattered the seed on the ground. Some fell on a path. Birds came and ate it up. [5]Some seed fell on rocky places, where there wasn't much soil. The plants came up quickly, because the soil wasn't deep. ⁶When the sun came up, it burned the plants. They dried up because they had no roots. ⁷Other seed fell among thorns. The thorns grew up and crowded out the plants. So the plants did not bear grain. ⁸Still other seed fell on good soil. It grew up and produced a crop 30, 60, or even 100 times more than the farmer planted."

⁹Then Jesus said, "Those who have ears should listen."

¹⁰Later Jesus was alone. The Twelve asked him about the stories. So did the others round him. ¹¹He told them, "The secret of God's kingdom has been given to you. But to outsiders everything is told by using stories. ¹²In this way,

" 'They will see but never know what they are seeing.
    They will hear but never understand.
  Otherwise they might turn and be forgiven!' " [ISAIAH 6:9,10]

¹³Then Jesus said to them, "Don't you understand this story? Then how will you understand any stories of this kind? ¹⁴The seed the farmer plants is God's message. ¹⁵What is seed scattered on a path like? The message is planted. The people hear the message. Then Satan comes. He takes away the message that was planted in them. ¹⁶And what is seed scattered on rocky places like? The people hear the message and at once receive it with joy. ¹⁷But they have no roots. So they last only a short time. They quickly fall away from the faith when trouble or suffering comes because of the message. ¹⁸And what is seed scattered among thorns like? The people hear the message. ¹⁹But then the worries of this life come to them. Wealth comes with its false promises. The people also long for other things. All these are the kinds of things that crowd out

the message. They keep it from producing fruit. ²⁰And what is seed scattered on good soil like? The people hear the message. They accept it. They produce a good crop 30, 60, or even 100 times more than the farmer planted."

A Lamp on a Stand

²¹Jesus said to them, "Do you bring in a lamp to put it under a large bowl or a bed? Don't you put it on its stand? ²²What is hidden is meant to be seen. And what is put out of sight is meant to be brought out into the open. ²³Everyone who has ears should listen."

²⁴"Think carefully about what you hear," he said. "As you give, so you will receive. In fact, you will receive even more. ²⁵If you have something, you will be given more. If you have nothing, even what you have will be taken away from you."

The Story of the Growing Seed

²⁶Jesus also said, "Here is what God's kingdom is like. A farmer scatters seed on the ground. ²⁷Night and day the seed comes up and grows. It happens whether the farmer sleeps or gets up. He doesn't know how it happens. ²⁸All by itself the soil produces corn. First the stalk comes up. Then the ear appears. Finally, the full corn appears in the ear. ²⁹Before long the corn ripens. So the farmer cuts it down, because the harvest is ready."

The Story of the Mustard Seed

³⁰Again Jesus said, "What can we say God's kingdom is like? What story can we use to explain it? ³¹It is like a mustard seed, which is the smallest seed planted in the ground. ³²But when you plant the seed, it grows. It becomes the largest of all

garden plants. Its branches are so big that birds can rest in its shade."

³³Using many stories like those, Jesus spoke the word to them. He told them as much as they could understand. ³⁴He did not say anything to them without using a story. But when he was alone with his disciples, he explained everything.

Jesus Calms the Storm

³⁵When evening came, Jesus said to his disciples, "Let's go over to the other side of the lake." ³⁶They left the crowd behind. And they took him along in a boat, just as he was. There were also other boats with him.

³⁷A wild storm came up. Waves crashed over the boat. It was about to sink. ³⁸Jesus was in the back, sleeping on a cushion. The disciples woke him up. They said, "Teacher! Don't you care if we drown?"

³⁹He got up and ordered the wind to stop. He said to the waves, "Quiet! Be still!" Then the wind died down. And it was completely calm.

⁴⁰He said to his disciples, "Why are you so afraid? Don't you have any faith at all yet?"

⁴¹They were terrified. They asked each other, "Who is this? Even the wind and the waves obey him!"

Jesus Heals a Man Controlled by Demons

5 They went across the Sea of Galilee to the area of the Gerasenes. ²Jesus got out of the boat. A man with an evil spirit came from the tombs to meet him. ³The man lived in the tombs. No-one could keep him tied up any more. Not even a chain could hold him. ⁴His hands and feet had often been chained. But he tore the chains apart. And he broke the iron chains on his ankles. No-one was strong enough to control him. [5]Night and day he screamed among the tombs and in the hills. He cut himself with stones.

[6]When he saw Jesus a long way off, he ran to him. He fell on his knees in front of him. [7]He shouted at the top of his voice, "Jesus, Son of the Most High God, what do you want with me? Promise before God that you won't hurt me!" [8]This was because Jesus had said to him, "Come out of this man, you evil spirit!"

[9]Then Jesus asked the demon, "What is your name?"

"My name is Legion," he replied. "There are many of us." [10]And he begged Jesus again and again not to send them out of the area.

[11]A large herd of pigs was feeding on the nearby hillside. [12]The demons begged Jesus, "Send us among the pigs. Let us go into them." [13]Jesus allowed it. The evil spirits came out of the man and went into the pigs. There were about 2,000 pigs in the herd. The whole herd rushed down the steep bank. They ran into the lake and drowned.

[14]Those who were tending the pigs ran off. They told the people in the town and countryside what had happened. The people went out to see for themselves.

[15]Then they came to Jesus. They saw the man who had been controlled by many demons. He was sitting there. He was now dressed and thinking clearly. All this made the people afraid. [16]Those who had seen it told them what had happened to the man. They told about the pigs as well. [17]Then the people began to beg Jesus to leave their area.

[18]Jesus was getting into the boat. The man who had been controlled by demons begged to go with him. [19]Jesus did not let him. He said, "Go home to your family. Tell them how much the Lord has done for you. Tell them how kind he has been to you."

20So the man went away. In the area known as the Ten Cities, he began to tell how much Jesus had done for him. And all the people were amazed.

A Dying Girl and a Suffering Woman

21Jesus went across the Sea of Galilee in a boat. It landed at the other side. There a large crowd gathered around him. 22Then a man named Jairus came. He was a synagogue ruler. Seeing Jesus, he fell at his feet. 23He begged Jesus, "Please come. My little daughter is dying. Place your hands on her to heal her. Then she will live." 24So Jesus went with him.

A large group of people followed. They crowded round him. 25A woman was there who had an illness that made her bleed. It had lasted for 12 years. 26She had suffered a great deal, even though she had gone to many doctors. She had spent all the money she had. But she was getting worse, not better. 27Then she heard about Jesus. She came up behind him in the crowd and touched his clothes. 28She thought, "I just need to touch his clothes. Then I will be healed." 29At once her bleeding stopped. She felt in her body that her suffering was over.

30At once Jesus knew that power had gone out from him. He turned around in the crowd. He asked, "Who touched my clothes?"

31"You see the people," his disciples answered. "They are crowding against you. And you still ask, 'Who touched me?'"

32But Jesus kept looking round. He wanted to see who had touched him.

33Then the woman came and fell at his feet. She knew what had happened to her. She was shaking with fear. But she told him the whole truth.

34He said to her, "Dear woman, your faith has healed you. Go in peace. You are free from your suffering."

³⁵While Jesus was still speaking, some people came from the house of Jairus. He was the synagogue ruler. "Your daughter is dead," they said. "Why bother the teacher any more?"

³⁶But Jesus didn't listen to them. He told the synagogue ruler, "Don't be afraid. Just believe."

³⁷He let only Peter, James, and John, the brother of James, follow him. ³⁸They came to the home of the synagogue ruler. There Jesus saw a lot of confusion. People were crying and weeping loudly. ³⁹He went inside. Then he said to them, "Why all this confusion and crying? The child is not dead. She is only sleeping." ⁴⁰But they laughed at him.

He made them all go outside. He took only the child's father and mother and the disciples who were with him. And he went in where the child was. ⁴¹He took her by the hand. Then he said to her, "*Talitha koum!*" This means, "Little girl, I say to you, get up!" ⁴²The girl was 12 years old. At once she stood up and walked around. They were totally amazed at this. ⁴³Jesus gave strict orders not to let anyone know what had happened. And he told them to give her something to eat.

A Prophet Without Honour

6 Jesus left there and went to his home town of Nazareth. His disciples went with him. ²When the Sabbath day came, he began to teach in the synagogue. Many who heard him were amazed.

"Where did this man get these things?" they asked. "What's this wisdom that has been given to him? He even does miracles! ³Isn't this the carpenter? Isn't this Mary's son? Isn't this the brother of James, Joseph, Judas and Simon? Aren't his sisters here with us?" They were not pleased with him at all.

⁴Jesus said to them, "A prophet is not honoured in his home

town. He doesn't receive any honour among his relatives. And he doesn't receive any in his own home."

⁵Jesus laid his hands on a few people who were ill and healed them. But he could not do any other miracles there. ⁶He was amazed because they had no faith.

Jesus Sends Out the Twelve Disciples

Jesus went round teaching from village to village. ⁷He called the Twelve to him. Then he sent them out two by two. He gave them authority to drive out evil spirits.

⁸Here were his orders. "Take only a walking stick for your trip. Do not take bread or a bag. Take no money in your belts. ⁹Wear sandals. But do not take extra clothes. ¹⁰When you are invited into a house, stay there until you leave town. ¹¹Some places may not welcome you or listen to you. If they don't, shake the dust off your feet when you leave. That will be a witness against the people living there."

¹²They went out. And they preached that people should turn away from their sins. ¹³They drove out many demons. They poured olive oil on many people who were ill and healed them.

John the Baptist's Head Is Cut Off

¹⁴King Herod heard about this. Jesus' name had become well known. Some were saying, "John the Baptist has been raised from the dead! That is why he has the power to do miracles."

¹⁵Others said, "He is Elijah."

Still others claimed, "He is a prophet. He is like one of the prophets of long ago."

¹⁶But when Herod heard this, he said, "I had John's head cut off. And now he has been raised from the dead!"

¹⁷In fact, it was Herod himself who had given orders to arrest

John. He had him tied up and put in prison. He did this because of Herodias. She was the wife of Herod's brother Philip. But now Herod was married to her. ¹⁸John had been saying to Herod, "It is against the law for you to have your brother's wife." ¹⁹Herodias held that against John. She wanted to kill him. But she could not, ²⁰because Herod was afraid of John. So he kept John safe. Herod knew John was a holy man who did what was right. When Herod heard him, he was very puzzled. But he liked to listen to him.

²¹Finally the right time came. Herod gave a big party on his birthday. He invited his high officials and military leaders. He also invited the most important men in Galilee. ²²Then the daughter of Herodias came in and danced. She pleased Herod and his dinner guests.

The king said to the girl, "Ask me for anything you want. I'll give it to you." ²³And he promised her with an oath, "Anything you ask for I will give you. I'll give you up to half of my kingdom."

²⁴She went out and said to her mother, "What should I ask for?"

"The head of John the Baptist," she answered.

²⁵At once the girl hurried to ask the king. She said, "I want you to give me the head of John the Baptist on a big plate here and now."

²⁶The king was very upset. But he thought of his promise and his dinner guests. So he did not want to say no to the girl. ²⁷He sent a man right away to bring John's head. The man went to the prison and cut off John's head. ²⁸He brought it back on a big plate. He gave it to the girl, and she gave it to her mother.

²⁹John's disciples heard about this. So they came and took his body. Then they placed it in a tomb.

Jesus Feeds the Five Thousand

³⁰The apostles gathered round Jesus. They told him all they had done and taught. ³¹But many people were coming and going. So they did not even have a chance to eat.

Then Jesus said to his apostles, "Come with me by yourselves to a quiet place. You need to get some rest." ³²So they went away by themselves in a boat to a quiet place.

³³But many people who saw them leaving recognised them. They ran from all the towns and got there ahead of them. ³⁴When Jesus came ashore, he saw a large crowd. He felt deep concern for them. They were like sheep without a shepherd. So he began teaching them many things.

³⁵By that time it was late in the day. His disciples came to him. "There is nothing here," they said. "It's already very late. ³⁶Send the people away. They can go and buy something to eat in the nearby countryside and villages."

³⁷But Jesus answered, "You give them something to eat."

They said to him, "That would take eight months of a person's pay! Should we go and spend that much on bread? Are we supposed to feed them?"

³⁸"How many loaves do you have?" Jesus asked. "Go and see."

When they found out, they said, "Five loaves and two fish."

³⁹Then Jesus directed them to make all the people sit down in groups on the green grass. ⁴⁰So they sat down in groups of 100s and 50s.

⁴¹Jesus took the five loaves and the two fish. He looked up to heaven and gave thanks. He broke the loaves into pieces. Then he gave them to his disciples to set in front of the people. He also divided the two fish among them all.

⁴²All of them ate and were satisfied. ⁴³The disciples picked up 12 baskets of broken pieces of bread and fish. ⁴⁴The number of men who had eaten was 5,000.

Jesus Walks on the Water

⁴⁵At once Jesus made his disciples get into the boat. He made them go on ahead of him to Bethsaida. Then he sent the crowd away. ⁴⁶After leaving them, he went up on a mountainside to pray.

⁴⁷When evening came, the boat was in the middle of the Sea of Galilee. Jesus was alone on land. ⁴⁸He saw the disciples pulling hard on the oars. The wind was blowing against them.

Early in the morning, he went out to them. He walked on the lake. When he was about to pass by them, ⁴⁹they saw him walking on the lake. They thought he was a ghost. They cried out. ⁵⁰They all saw him and were terrified.

At once he said to them, "Be brave! It is I. Don't be afraid."

⁵¹Then he climbed into the boat with them. The wind died down. And they were completely amazed. ⁵²They had not understood about the loaves. They were stubborn.

⁵³They crossed over the lake and landed at Gennesaret. There they tied up the boat. ⁵⁴As soon as Jesus and his disciples got out, people recognised him. ⁵⁵They ran through that whole area to bring to him those who were ill. They carried them on mats to where they heard he was.

⁵⁶He went into the villages, the towns, and the countryside. Everywhere he went, the people brought people who were ill to the market-places. Those who were ill begged him to let them touch just the edge of his clothes. And all who touched him were healed.

What Makes People "Unclean"?

7 The Pharisees gathered around Jesus. So did some of the teachers of the law. All of them had come from Jerusalem. ²They saw some of his disciples eating food with "unclean" hands. That means they were not washed.

³The Pharisees and all the Jews do not eat unless they wash their hands to make them pure. This is what the elders teach. ⁴When they come from the market-place, they do not eat unless they wash. And they follow many other teachings. For example, they wash cups, jugs and kettles in a special way.

⁵So the Pharisees and the teachers of the law questioned Jesus. "Why don't your disciples live by what the elders teach?" they asked. "Why do they eat their food with 'unclean' hands?"

⁶He replied, "Isaiah was right. He prophesied about you people who pretend to be good. He said,

" 'These people honour me by what they say.
    But their hearts are far away from me.
⁷Their worship doesn't mean anything to me.
    They teach nothing but human rules.' [ISAIAH 29:13]

⁸You have let go of God's commands. And you are holding on to the teachings that men have made up."

⁹Jesus then said to them, "You have a fine way of setting aside God's commands! You do this so you can follow your own teachings. ¹⁰Moses said, 'Honour your father and mother.' [EXODUS 20:12; DEUTERONOMY 5:16] He also said, 'If anyone calls down a curse on his father or mother, he will be put to death.' [EXODUS 21:17; LEVITICUS 20:9] ¹¹But you allow people to say to their parents, 'Any help you might have received from us is Corban.' (Corban means 'a gift set apart for God'.) ¹²So you no longer let them do anything for their parents. ¹³You make the

word of God useless by putting your own teachings in its place. And you do many things like that."

[14]Again Jesus called the crowd to him. He said, "Listen to me, everyone. Understand this. [15/16]Nothing outside you can make you 'unclean' by going into you. It is what comes out of you that makes you 'unclean'."

[17]Then he left the crowd and entered the house. His disciples asked him about this teaching.

[18]"Don't you understand?" Jesus asked. "Don't you see? Nothing that enters people from the outside can make them 'unclean'. [19]It doesn't go into the heart. It goes into the stomach. Then it goes out of the body." In saying this, Jesus was calling all foods "clean".

[20]He went on to say, "What comes out of people makes them 'unclean'. [21]Evil thoughts come from the inside, from people's hearts. So do sexual sins, stealing and murder. Adultery, [22]greed, hate and cheating come from people's hearts too. So do desires that are not pure, and wanting what belongs to others. And so do telling lies about others and being proud and being foolish. [23]All these evil things come from inside a person. They make him 'unclean'."

The Faith of a Greek Woman

[24]Jesus went from there to a place near Tyre. He entered a house. He did not want anyone to know where he was. But he could not keep it a secret.

[25]Soon a woman heard about him. An evil spirit controlled her little daughter. The woman came to Jesus and fell at his feet. [26]She was a Greek, born in Syrian Phoenicia. She begged Jesus to drive the demon out of her daughter.

[27]"First let the children eat all they want," he told her. "It is not right to take the children's bread and throw it to their dogs."

28"Yes, Lord," she replied. "But even the dogs under the table eat the children's crumbs."

29Then he told her, "That was a good reply. You may go. The demon has left your daughter."

30So she went home and found her child lying on the bed. And the demon was gone.

Jesus Heals a Man Who Could Not Hear or Speak

31Then Jesus left the area of Tyre and went through Sidon. He went down to the Sea of Galilee and into the area known as the Ten Cities.

32There some people brought a man to him. The man was deaf and could hardly speak. They begged Jesus to place his hand on him.

33Jesus took the man to one side, away from the crowd. He put his fingers into the man's ears. Then he spat and touched the man's tongue. 34Jesus looked up to heaven. With a deep sigh, he said to the man, "*Ephphatha*!" That means "Be opened!" 35The man's ears were opened. His tongue was set free, and he began to speak clearly.

36Jesus ordered the people not to tell anyone. But the more he did so, the more they kept talking about it.

37People were really amazed. "He has done everything well," they said. "He even makes deaf people able to hear. And he makes those who can't speak able to talk."

Jesus Feeds the Four Thousand

8 During those days another large crowd gathered. They had nothing to eat. So Jesus called for his disciples to come to him. He said, 2"I feel deep concern for these people. They have already been with me three days. They don't have anything to eat. 3If I send them away hungry, they will become too weak on their way home. Some of them have come from far away."

⁴His disciples answered him, "There is nothing here," they said. "Where can anyone get enough bread to feed them?"

⁵"How many loaves do you have?" Jesus asked.

"Seven," they replied.

⁶He told the crowd to sit down on the ground. He took the seven loaves and gave thanks to God. Then he broke them and gave them to his disciples. They set the loaves down in front of the people. ⁷The disciples also had a few small fish. Jesus gave thanks for them too. He told the disciples to pass them round. ⁸The people ate and were satisfied.

After that, the disciples picked up seven baskets of leftover pieces. ⁹About 4,000 men were there. Jesus sent them away. ¹⁰Then he got into a boat with his disciples. He went to the area of Dalmanutha.

¹¹The Pharisees came and began to ask Jesus questions. They wanted to put him to the test. So they asked him for a miraculous sign from heaven. ¹²He sighed deeply. He said, "Why do you people ask for a sign? What I'm about to tell you is true. No sign will be given to you."

¹³Then he left them. He got back into the boat and crossed to the other side of the lake.

The Yeast of the Pharisees and Herod

¹⁴The disciples had forgotten to bring bread. They had only one loaf with them in the boat.

¹⁵"Be careful," Jesus warned them. "Watch out for the yeast of the Pharisees. And watch out for the yeast of Herod."

¹⁶They talked about this with each other. They said, "He must be saying this because we don't have any bread."

¹⁷Jesus knew what they were saying. So he asked them, "Why are you talking about having no bread? Why can't you see or understand? Are you stubborn? ¹⁸Do you have eyes and still don't see? Do you have ears and still don't hear? And don't you remember? ¹⁹Earlier I broke five loaves for the 5,000. How many baskets of pieces did you pick up?"

"Twelve," they replied.

²⁰"Later I broke seven loaves for the 4,000. How many baskets of pieces did you pick up?"

"Seven," they answered.

²¹He said to them, "Can't you understand yet?"

Jesus Heals a Blind Man

²²Jesus and his disciples came to Bethsaida. Some people brought a blind man. They begged Jesus to touch him.

²³He took the blind man by the hand. Then he led him outside the village. He spat on the man's eyes and put his hands on him.

"Do you see anything?" Jesus asked.

²⁴The man looked up. He said, "I see people. They look like trees walking around."

²⁵Once more Jesus put his hands on the man's eyes. Then his eyes were opened so that he could see again. He saw everything clearly.

²⁶Jesus sent him home. He told him, "Don't go into the village."

Peter Says That Jesus Is the Christ

²⁷Jesus and his disciples went on to the villages around Caesarea Philippi. On the way he asked them, "Who do people say I am?"

²⁸They replied, "Some say John the Baptist. Others say Elijah. Still others say one of the prophets."

²⁹"But what about you?" he asked. "Who do you say I am?" Peter answered, "You are the Christ."

³⁰Jesus warned them not to tell anyone about him.

Jesus Tells About His Coming Death

³¹Jesus then began to teach his disciples. He taught them that the Son of Man must suffer many things. He taught them that the elders would not accept him. The chief priests and the teachers of the law would not accept him either. He must be killed and after three days rise again. ³²He spoke clearly about this.

Peter took Jesus to one side and began to tell him off.

³³Jesus turned and looked at his disciples. He told Peter off. "Get behind me, Satan!" he said. "You are not thinking about the things of God. Instead, you are thinking about human things."

³⁴Jesus called the crowd to him along with his disciples. He said, "If anyone wants to come after me, he must say no to himself. He must pick up his cross and follow me. ³⁵If he wants to save his life, he will lose it. But if he loses his life for me and for the good news, he will save it. ³⁶What good is it if someone gains the whole world but loses his soul? ³⁷Or what can anyone exchange for his soul?

³⁸"Suppose you are ashamed of me and my words among these adulterous and sinful people. Then the Son of Man will be ashamed of you when he comes in his Father's glory with the holy angels."

9 Jesus said to them, "What I'm about to tell you is true. Some who are standing here will not die before they see God's kingdom coming with power."

Jesus' Appearance Is Changed

²After six days Jesus took Peter, James and John with him. He led them up a high mountain. They were all alone. There in front of them his appearance was changed. ³His clothes became so white that they shone. They were whiter than anyone in the world could bleach them. ⁴Elijah and Moses appeared in front of Jesus and his disciples. The two of them were talking with Jesus.

⁵Peter said to Jesus, "Rabbi, it is good for us to be here. Let us put up three shelters. One will be for you, one for Moses, and one for Elijah." ⁶Peter didn't really know what to say, because they were so afraid.

⁷Then a cloud appeared and surrounded them. A voice came from the cloud. It said, "This is my Son, and I love him. Listen to him!"

⁸They looked around. Suddenly they no longer saw anyone with them except Jesus.

⁹They came down the mountain. On the way down, Jesus ordered them not to tell anyone what they had seen. He told them to wait until the Son of Man had risen from the dead. ¹⁰So they kept the matter to themselves. But they asked each other what "rising from the dead" meant.

¹¹Then they asked Jesus, "Why do the teachers of the law say that Elijah has to come first?"

¹²Jesus replied, "That's right. Elijah does come first. He makes all things new again. So why is it written that the Son of Man must suffer much and not be accepted? ¹³I tell you, Elijah has come. They have done to him everything they wanted to do. They did it just as it is written about him."

Jesus Heals a Boy Who Had an Evil Spirit

[14]When Jesus and those who were with him came to the other disciples, they saw a large crowd around them. The teachers of the law were arguing with them. [15]When all the people saw Jesus, they were filled with wonder. And they ran to greet him.

[16]"What are you arguing with them about?" Jesus asked.

[17]A man in the crowd answered. "Teacher," he said, "I brought you my son. He is controlled by a spirit. Because of this, my son can't speak any more. [18]When the spirit takes hold of him, it throws him to the ground. He foams at the mouth. He grinds his teeth. And his body becomes stiff. I asked your disciples to drive out the spirit. But they couldn't do it."

[19]"You unbelieving people!" Jesus replied. "How long do I have to stay with you? How long do I have to put up with you? Bring the boy to me."

[20]So they brought him. As soon as the spirit saw Jesus, it threw the boy into a fit. He fell to the ground. He rolled around and foamed at the mouth.

[21]Jesus asked the boy's father, "How long has he been like this?"

"Since he was a child," he answered. [22]"The spirit has often thrown him into fire or water to kill him. But if you can do anything, take pity on us. Please help us."

[23]" 'If you can'?" said Jesus. "Everything is possible for the one who believes."

[24]Right away the boy's father cried out, "I do believe! Help me overcome my unbelief!"

[25]Jesus saw that a crowd was running over to see what was happening. Then he ordered the evil spirit to leave the boy.

"You spirit that makes him unable to hear and speak!" he said. "I command you, come out of him. Never enter him again."

²⁶The spirit screamed. It shook the boy wildly. Then it came out of him. The boy looked so lifeless that many people said, "He's dead." ²⁷But Jesus took him by the hand. He lifted the boy to his feet, and the boy stood up.

²⁸Jesus went indoors. Then his disciples asked him in private, "Why couldn't we drive out the evil spirit?"

²⁹He replied, "This kind can come out only by prayer."

³⁰They left that place and passed through Galilee. Jesus did not want anyone to know where they were. ³¹That was because he was teaching his disciples.

He said to them, "The Son of Man is going to be handed over to men. They will kill him. After three days he will rise from the dead." ³²But they didn't understand what he meant. And they were afraid to ask him about it.

Who Is the Most Important Person?

³³Jesus and his disciples came to a house in Capernaum. There he asked them, "What were you arguing about on the road?" ³⁴But they kept quiet. On the way, they had argued about which one of them was the most important person.

³⁵Jesus sat down and called for the Twelve to come to him. Then he said, "If you want to be first, you must be the very last. You must be the servant of everyone."

³⁶Jesus took a little child and made the child stand among them. Then he took the child in his arms. He said to them, ³⁷"Anyone who welcomes one of these little children in my name welcomes me. And anyone who welcomes me doesn't welcome only me but also the One who sent me."

Anyone Who Is Not Against Us Is for Us

38"Teacher," said John, "we saw a man driving out demons in your name. We told him to stop, because he was not one of us."

39"Do not stop him," Jesus said. "No-one who does a miracle in my name can in the next moment say anything bad about me. 40Anyone who is not against us is for us.

41"What I'm about to tell you is true. Suppose someone gives you a cup of water in my name because you belong to me. That one will certainly not go without a reward.

Leading People to Sin

42"What if someone leads one of these little ones who believe in me to sin? If he does, it would be better for him to be thrown into the sea with a large millstone tied round his neck.

43/44"If your hand causes you to sin, cut it off. It would be better for you to enter God's kingdom with only one hand than to go into hell with two hands. In hell the fire never goes out.

45/46"If your foot causes you to sin, cut it off. It would be better for you to enter God's kingdom with only one foot than to have two feet and be thrown into hell.

47"If your eye causes you to sin, poke it out. It would be better for you to enter God's kingdom with only one eye than to have two eyes and be thrown into hell. 48In hell,

" 'The worms do not die.
The fire is not put out.'

[ISAIAH 66:24]

⁴⁹Everyone will be salted with fire.

⁵⁰"Salt is good. But suppose it loses its saltiness. How can you make it salty again? Have salt in yourselves. And be at peace with each other."

Jesus Teaches About Divorce

10 Jesus left that place and went into the area of Judea and across the River Jordan. Again crowds of people came to him. As usual, he taught them.

²Some Pharisees came to put him to the test. They asked, "Does the Law allow a man to divorce his wife?"

³"What did Moses command you?" he replied.

⁴They said, "Moses allowed a man to write a letter of divorce and send her away."

⁵"You were stubborn. That's why Moses wrote you this law," Jesus replied. ⁶"But at the beginning of creation, God 'made them male and female'. [GENESIS 1:27] ⁷That's why a man will leave his father and mother and be joined to his wife. ⁸The two of them will become one.' [GENESIS 2:24] They are no longer two, but one. ⁹So a man must not separate what God has joined together."

¹⁰When they were in the house again, the disciples asked Jesus about this.

¹¹He answered, "What if a man divorces his wife and gets married to another woman? He commits adultery against her. ¹²And what if she divorces her husband and gets married to another man? She commits adultery."

Little Children Are Brought to Jesus

¹³People were bringing little children to Jesus. They wanted him to touch them. But the disciples told the people to stop.

¹⁴When Jesus saw this, he was angry. He said to his disciples,

"Let the little children come to me. Don't keep them away. God's kingdom belongs to people like them. ¹⁵What I'm about to tell you is true. Anyone who will not receive God's kingdom like a little child will never enter it."

¹⁶Then he took the children in his arms. He put his hands on them and blessed them.

Jesus and the Rich Young Man

¹⁷As Jesus started on his way, someone ran up to him. He fell on his knees before Jesus. "Good teacher," he said, "what must I do to receive eternal life?"

¹⁸"Why do you call me good?" Jesus answered. "No-one is good except God. ¹⁹You know what the commandments say. 'Do not commit murder. Do not commit adultery. Do not steal. Do not give false witness. Do not cheat. Honour your father and mother.'" [EXODUS 20:12–16; DEUTERONOMY 5:16–20]

²⁰"Teacher," he said, "I have obeyed all these commandments since I was a boy."

²¹Jesus looked at him and loved him. "You are missing one thing," he said. "Go and sell everything you have. Give the money to those who are poor. You will have treasure in heaven. Then come and follow me."

²²The man's face fell. He went away sad, because he was very rich.

²³Jesus looked around. He said to his disciples, "How hard it is for rich people to enter God's kingdom!"

²⁴The disciples were amazed at his words. But Jesus said again, "Children, how hard it is to enter God's kingdom! ²⁵Is it hard for a camel to go through the eye of a needle? It is even harder for the rich to enter God's kingdom!"

²⁶The disciples were even more amazed. They said to each other, "Then who can be saved?"

[27]Jesus looked at them and said, "With man, that is impossible. But not with God. All things are possible with God."

[28]Peter said to him, "We have left everything to follow you!"

[29]"What I'm about to tell you is true," Jesus replied. "Has anyone left home or family or fields for me and the good news? [30]They will receive 100 times as much in this world. They will have homes and families and fields. But they will also be treated badly by others. In the world to come they will live for ever. [31]But many who are first will be last. And the last will be first."

Jesus Again Tells About His Coming Death

[32]They were on their way up to Jerusalem. Jesus was leading the way. The disciples were amazed. Those who followed were afraid.

Again Jesus took the Twelve to one side. He told them what was going to happen to him. [33]"We are going up to Jerusalem," he said. "The Son of Man will be handed over to the chief priests and the teachers of the law. They will sentence him to death. Then they will hand him over to people who are not Jews. [34]The people will make fun of him and spit on him. They will flog him and kill him. Three days later he will rise from the dead!"

James and John Ask a Favour of Jesus

[35]James and John came to Jesus. They were the sons of Zebedee. "Teacher," they said, "we would like to ask a favour of you."

[36]"What do you want me to do for you?" he asked.

[37]They replied, "Let one of us sit at your right hand in your glorious kingdom. Let the other one sit at your left hand."

[38]"You don't know what you're asking for," Jesus said. "Can

you drink the cup of suffering I drink? Or can you go through the baptism of suffering I must go through?"

[39]"We can," they answered.

Jesus said to them, "You will drink the cup I drink. And you will go through the baptism I go through. [40]But it is not for me to say who will sit at my right or left hand. These places belong to those they are prepared for."

[41]The other ten disciples heard about it. They became angry at James and John.

[42]Jesus called them together. He said, "You know about those who are rulers of the nations. They hold power over their people. Their high officials order them around. [43]Don't be like that. Instead, anyone who wants to be important among you must be your servant. [44]And anyone who wants to be first must be the slave of everyone. [45]Even the Son of Man did not come to be served. Instead, he came to serve others. He came to give his life as the price for setting many people free."

Blind Bartimaeus Receives His Sight

[46]Jesus and his disciples came to Jericho. They were leaving the city. A large crowd was with them.

A blind man was sitting by the side of the road begging. His name was Bartimaeus. Bartimaeus means Son of Timaeus. [47]He heard that Jesus of Nazareth was passing by. So he began to shout, "Jesus! Son of David! Have mercy on me!"

[48]Many people commanded him to stop. They told him to be quiet. But he shouted even louder, "Son of David! Have mercy on me!"

[49]Jesus stopped and said, "Call for him."

So they called out to the blind man, "Cheer up! Get up on your feet! Jesus is calling for you."

⁵⁰He threw his coat to one side. Then he jumped to his feet and came to Jesus.

⁵¹"What do you want me to do for you?" Jesus asked him. The blind man said, "Rabbi, I want to be able to see."

⁵²"Go," said Jesus. "Your faith has healed you."

At once he could see. And he followed Jesus along the road.

Jesus Enters Jerusalem

11 As they all approached Jerusalem, they came to Bethphage and Bethany at the Mount of Olives. Jesus sent out two of his disciples. ²He said to them, "Go to the village ahead of you. Just as you enter it, you will find a donkey's colt tied there. No-one has ever ridden it. Untie it and bring it here. ³Someone may ask you, 'Why are you doing this?' If so, say, 'The Lord needs it. But he will send it back here soon.'"

⁴So they left. They found a colt out in the street. It was tied at a doorway. They untied it. ⁵Some people standing there asked, "What are you doing? Why are you untying that colt?" ⁶They answered as Jesus had told them to. So the people let them go.

⁷They brought the colt to Jesus. They threw their coats over it. Then he sat on it.

⁸Many people spread their coats on the road. Others spread branches they had cut in the fields. ⁹Those in front and those at the back shouted,

"Hosanna!"

"Blessed is the one who comes in the name of the Lord!"
[PSALM 118:25,26]

[10]"Blessed is the coming kingdom of our father David!"

"Hosanna in the highest heaven!"

[11]Jesus entered Jerusalem and went to the temple. He looked around at everything. But it was already late. So he went out to Bethany with the Twelve.

Jesus Clears the Temple

[12]The next day as Jesus and his disciples were leaving Bethany, they were hungry. [13]Not too far away, he saw a fig-tree. It was covered with leaves. He went to find out if it had any fruit. When he reached it, he found nothing but leaves. It was not the season for figs.

[14]Then Jesus said to the tree, "May no-one ever eat fruit from you again!" And his disciples heard him say it.

[15]When Jesus reached Jerusalem, he entered the temple area. He began chasing out those who were buying and selling there. He turned over the tables of the people who were exchanging money. He also turned over the benches of those who were selling doves. [16]He would not allow anyone to carry items for sale through the temple courts.

[17]Then he taught them. He told them, "It is written that the Lord said,

" 'My house will be called
   a house where people from all nations can pray'
   [ISAIAH 56:7]

But you have made it 'a den for robbers'." [JEREMIAH 7:11]

[18]The chief priests and the teachers of the law heard about this. They began looking for a way to kill Jesus. They were

afraid of him, because the whole crowd was amazed at his teaching.

¹⁹When evening came, Jesus and his disciples left the city.

The Dried-up Fig-Tree

²⁰In the morning as Jesus and his disciples walked along, they saw the fig-tree. It was dried up all the way down to the roots.

²¹Peter remembered. He said to Jesus, "Rabbi, look! The fig-tree you put a curse on has dried up!"

²²"Have faith in God," Jesus said. ²³"What I'm about to tell you is true. Suppose one of you says to this mountain, 'Go and throw yourself into the sea.' You must not doubt in your heart. You must believe that what you say will happen. Then it will be done for you.

²⁴"So I tell you, when you pray for something, believe that you have already received it. Then it will be yours. ^{25/26}And when you stand praying, forgive anyone you have anything against. Then your Father in heaven will forgive your sins."

The Authority of Jesus Is Questioned

²⁷Jesus and his disciples arrived again in Jerusalem. He was walking in the temple courts. Then the chief priests came to him. The teachers of the law and the elders came too.

²⁸"By what authority are you doing these things?" they asked. "Who gave you authority to do this?"

²⁹Jesus replied, "I will ask you one question. Answer me, and I will tell you by what authority I am doing these things. ³⁰Was John's baptism from heaven? Or did it come from men? Tell me!"

³¹They talked to each other about it. They said, "If we say, 'From heaven', he will ask, 'Then why didn't you believe him?'

³²But what if we say, 'From men'?" They were afraid of the people. Everyone believed that John really was a prophet.

³³So they answered Jesus, "We don't know."

Jesus said, "Then I won't tell you by what authority I am doing these things either."

The Story of the Renters

12 Jesus began to speak to the people by using stories. He said, "A man planted a vineyard. He put a wall around it. He dug a pit for a winepress. He also built a watchtower. He let the vineyard out to some farmers. Then he went away on a journey.

²"At harvest time he sent a servant to the tenants. He told the servant to collect from them some of the fruit of the vineyard. ³But they grabbed the servant and beat him up. Then they sent him away with nothing. ⁴So the man sent another servant to the tenants. They hit this one on the head and treated him badly. ⁵The man sent still another servant. The tenants killed him. The man sent many others. The tenants beat up some of them. They killed the others.

⁶"The man had one person left to send. It was his son, and he loved him. He sent him last of all. He said, 'They will respect my son.'

⁷"But the tenants said to each other, 'This is the one who will receive all the owner's property some day. Come, let's kill him. Then everything will be ours.' ⁸So they took him and killed him. They threw him out of the vineyard.

⁹"What will the owner of the vineyard do then? He will come and kill those tenants. He will give the vineyard to others.

¹⁰"Haven't you read what Scripture says,

" 'The stone the builders didn't accept
has become the most important stone of all.
¹¹The Lord has done it.
It is wonderful in our eyes'?"

[PSALM 118:22,23]

¹²Then the religious leaders looked for a way to arrest Jesus. They knew he had told the story against them. But they were afraid of the crowd. So they left him and went away.

Is It Right to Pay Taxes to Caesar?

¹³Later the religious leaders sent some of the Pharisees and Herodians to Jesus. They wanted to trap him with his own words.

¹⁴They came to him and said, "Teacher, we know you are a person of honour. You don't let others tell you what to do or say. You don't care how important they are. But you teach the way of God truthfully. Is it right to pay taxes to Caesar or not? ¹⁵Should we pay or shouldn't we?"

But Jesus knew what they were trying to do. So he asked, "Why are you trying to trap me? Bring me a silver coin. Let me look at it."

¹⁶They brought the coin.

He asked them, "Whose picture is this? And whose words?"

"Caesar's," they replied.

¹⁷Then Jesus said to them, "Give to Caesar what belongs to Caesar. And give to God what belongs to God."

They were amazed at him.

Marriage When the Dead Rise

¹⁸The Sadducees came to Jesus with a question. They do not believe that people rise from the dead. ¹⁹"Teacher," they said,

"Moses wrote for us about a man who died and didn't have any children. But he did leave a wife behind. That man's brother must get married to the widow. He must have children to carry on his dead brother's name.

20"There were seven brothers. The first one got married. He died without leaving any children. 21The second one got married to the widow. He also died and left no child. It was the same with the third one. 22In fact, none of the seven left any children. Last of all, the woman died too. 23When the dead rise, whose wife will she be? All seven of them were married to her."

24Jesus replied, "You are mistaken, because you do not know the Scriptures. And you do not know the power of God. 25When the dead rise, they won't get married. And their parents won't give them to be married. They will be like the angels in heaven.

26"What about the dead rising? Haven't you read in the scroll of Moses the story of the bush? God said to Moses, 'I am the God of Abraham. I am the God of Isaac. And I am the God of Jacob.' [EXODUS 3:6] 27He is not the God of the dead. He is the God of the living. You have made a big mistake!"

The Most Important Commandment

28One of the teachers of the law came and heard the Sadducees arguing. He noticed that Jesus had given the Sadducees a good answer. So he asked him, "Which is the most important of all the commandments?"

29Jesus answered, "Here is the most important one. Moses said, 'Israel, listen to me. The Lord is our God. The Lord is one. 30Love the Lord your God with all your heart and with all your soul. Love him with all your mind and with all your strength.' [DEUTERONOMY 6:4,5] 31And here is the second one. 'Love your neighbour as you love yourself.' [LEVITICUS 19:18] There is no commandment more important than these."

³²"You have spoken well, teacher," the man replied. "You are right in saying that God is one. There is no other God but him. ³³To love God with all your heart and mind and strength is very important. So is loving your neighbour as you love yourself. These things are more important than all burnt offerings and sacrifices."

³⁴Jesus saw that the man had answered wisely. He said to him, "You are not far from God's kingdom."

From then on, no-one dared to ask Jesus any more questions.

Whose Son Is the Christ?

³⁵Jesus was teaching in the temple courts. He asked, "Why do the teachers of the law say that the Christ is the son of David? ³⁶The Holy Spirit spoke through David himself. David said,

" 'The Lord said to my Lord,
   "Sit at my right hand
until I put your enemies
   under your control." '

[PSALM 110:1]

³⁷David himself calls him 'Lord'. So how can he be David's son?"

The large crowd listened to Jesus with delight.

³⁸As he taught, he said, "Watch out for the teachers of the law. They like to walk around in long robes. They like to be greeted in the market-places. ³⁹They love to have the most important seats in the synagogues. They also love to have the

places of honour at dinners. [40]They take over the houses of widows. They say long prayers to show off. God will punish those men very much."

The Widow's Offering

[41]Jesus sat down opposite the place where people put their temple offerings. He watched the crowd putting their money into the offering boxes. Many rich people threw large amounts into them.

[42]But a poor widow came and put in two very small copper coins. They were worth much less than a penny.

[43]Jesus asked his disciples to come to him. He said, "What I'm about to tell you is true. This poor widow has put more into the offering box than all the others. [44]They all gave a lot because they are rich. But she gave even though she is poor. She put in everything she had. She gave all she had to live on."

Signs of the End

13 Jesus was leaving the temple. One of his disciples said to him, "Look, Teacher! What huge stones! What wonderful buildings!"

[2]"Do you see these huge buildings?" Jesus asked. "Not one stone here will be left on top of another. Every stone will be thrown down."

[3]Jesus was sitting on the Mount of Olives, opposite the temple. Peter, James, John and Andrew asked him a question in private. [4]"Tell us," they said. "When will these things happen? And what will be the sign that they are all about to come true?"

[5]Jesus said to them, "Keep watch! Be careful that no-one fools you. [6]Many will come in my name. They will claim, 'I am he.' They will fool many people.

[7]"You will hear about wars. You will also hear people talking about future wars. Don't be alarmed. Those things must happen. But the end still isn't here. [8]Nation will fight against nation. Kingdom will fight against kingdom. There will be earthquakes in many places. People will go hungry. All these things are the beginning of birth-pains.

[9]"Watch out! You will be handed over to the local courts. You will be flogged in the synagogues. You will stand in front of governors and kings because of me. In that way you will be witnesses to them. [10]The good news has to be preached to all nations before the end comes. [11]You will be arrested and brought to trial. But don't worry ahead of time about what you will say. Just say what God brings to your mind at the time. It is not you speaking, but the Holy Spirit.

[12]"Brothers will hand over brothers to be killed. Fathers will hand over their children. Children will rise up against their parents and have them put to death. [13]Everyone will hate you because of me. But the one who stands firm to the end will be saved.

[14]"You will see 'the hated thing that destroys'. [DANIEL 9:27; 11:31; 12:11] It will stand where it does not belong. The reader should understand this. Then those who are in Judea should escape to the mountains. [15]No-one on the roof should go down into his house to take anything out. [16]No-one in the field should go back to get his coat. [17]How awful it will be in those days for pregnant women! How awful for nursing mothers! [18]Pray that this will not happen in winter.

[19]"Those days will be worse than any others from the time God created the world until now. And there will never be any like them again. [20]If the Lord had not cut the time short, no-one would live. But because of God's chosen people, he has shortened it.

²¹"At that time someone may say to you, 'Look! Here is the Christ!' Or, 'Look! There he is!' Do not believe it. ²²False Christs and false prophets will appear. They will do signs and miracles. They will try to fool God's chosen people if possible. ²³Keep watch! I have told you everything ahead of time.

²⁴"So in those days there will be terrible suffering, After that, Scripture says,

" 'The sun will be darkened.
   The moon will not shine.
²⁵The stars will fall from the sky.
   The heavenly bodies will be shaken.' [ISAIAH 13:10; 34:4]

²⁶"At that time people will see the Son of Man coming in clouds. He will come with great power and glory. ²⁷He will send his angels. He will gather his chosen people from all four directions. He will bring them from the ends of the earth to the ends of the heavens.

²⁸"Learn a lesson from the fig-tree. As soon as its twigs get tender and its leaves come out, you know that summer is near. ²⁹In the same way, when you see these things happening, you will know that the end is near. It is right at the door. ³⁰What I'm about to tell you is true. The people living at that time will certainly not pass away until all these things have happened. ³¹Heaven and earth will pass away. But my words will never pass away.

The Day and Hour Are Not Known

³²"No-one knows about the day or hour. Not even the angels in heaven know. The Son does not know. Only the Father knows.

[33]"Keep watch! Stay awake! You do not know when that time will come. [34]It's like a man going away. He leaves his house and puts his servants in charge. Each one is given a task to do. He tells the one at the door to keep watch.

[35]"So keep watch! You do not know when the owner of the house will come back. It may be in the evening or at midnight. It may be when the cock crows or at dawn. [36]He may come suddenly. So do not let him find you sleeping.

[37]"What I say to you, I say to everyone. 'Watch!' "

A Woman Pours Perfume on Jesus

14 The Passover and the Feast of Unleavened Bread were only two days away. The chief priests and the teachers of the law were looking for a clever way to arrest Jesus. They wanted to kill him. [2]"But not during the Feast," they said. "The people may stir up trouble."

[3]Jesus was in Bethany. He was at the table in the home of a man named Simon, who had a skin disease. A woman came with a special sealed jar of very expensive perfume. It was made out of pure nard. She broke the jar open and poured the perfume on Jesus' head.

[4]Some of the people there became angry. They said to one another, "Why waste this perfume? [5]It could have been sold for more than a year's pay. The money could have been given to poor people." So they found fault with the woman.

[6]"Leave her alone," Jesus said. "Why are you bothering her? She has done a beautiful thing to me. [7]You will always have poor people with you. You can help them any time you want to. But you will not always have me. [8]She did what she could. She poured perfume on my body to prepare me to be buried. [9]What I'm about to tell you is true. What she has done will be

told anywhere the good news is preached all over the world. It will be told in memory of her."

¹⁰Judas Iscariot was one of the Twelve. He went to the chief priests to hand Jesus over to them. ¹¹They were delighted to hear that he would do this. They promised to give Judas money. So he watched for the right time to hand Jesus over to them.

The Lord's Supper

¹²It was the first day of the Feast of Unleavened Bread. That was the time to sacrifice the Passover lamb.

Jesus' disciples asked him, "Where do you want us to go and prepare for you to eat the Passover meal?"

¹³So he sent out two of his disciples. He told them, "Go into the city. A man carrying a jar of water will meet you. Follow him. ¹⁴He will enter a house. Say to its owner, 'The Teacher asks, "Where is my guest room? Where can I eat the Passover meal with my disciples?"' ¹⁵He will show you a large upstairs room. It will have furniture and will be ready. Prepare for us to eat there."

¹⁶The disciples left and went into the city. They found things just as Jesus had told them. So they prepared the Passover meal.

¹⁷When evening came, Jesus arrived with the Twelve. ¹⁸While they were at the table eating, Jesus said, "What I'm about to tell you is true. One of you who is eating with me will hand me over to my enemies."

¹⁹The disciples became sad. One by one they said to him, "It's not I, is it?"

²⁰"It is one of the Twelve," Jesus replied. "It is the one who dips bread into the bowl with me. ²¹The Son of Man will go just as it is written about him. But how terrible it will be for the

one who hands over the Son of Man! It would be better for him if he had not been born."

²²While they were eating, Jesus took bread. He gave thanks and broke it. He handed it to his disciples and said, "Take it. This is my body."

²³Then he took the cup. He gave thanks and handed it to them. All of them drank from it.

²⁴"This is my blood of the new covenant," he said to them. "It is poured out for many. ²⁵What I'm about to tell you is true. I won't drink from the fruit of the vine until the day I drink it again in God's kingdom."

²⁶Then they sang a hymn and went out to the Mount of Olives.

Jesus Says That Peter Will Fail

²⁷"You will all turn away," Jesus told the disciples. "It is written,

" 'I will strike the shepherd down.
     Then the sheep will be scattered.' [ZECHARIAH 13:7]

²⁸But after I rise from the dead, I will go ahead of you into Galilee."

²⁹Peter said, "All the others may turn away. But I will not."

³⁰"What I'm about to tell you is true," Jesus answered. "It will happen today, this very night. Before the cock crows twice, you yourself will say three times that you don't know me."

³¹But Peter would not give in. He said, "I may have to die with you. But I will never say I don't know you." And all the others said the same thing.

Jesus Prays in Gethsemane

³²Jesus and his disciples went to a place called Gethsemane. Jesus said to them, "Sit here while I pray."

³³He took Peter, James and John along with him. He began to be very upset and troubled. ³⁴"My soul is very sad. I feel close to death," he said to them. "Stay here. Keep watch."

³⁵He went a little farther. Then he fell to the ground. He prayed that, if possible, the hour might pass by him. ³⁶"*Abba*," he said, "everything is possible for you. Take this cup of suffering away from me. But let what you want be done, not what I want." *Abba* means Father.

³⁷Then he returned to his disciples and found them sleeping. "Simon," he said to Peter, "are you asleep? Couldn't you keep watch for one hour? ³⁸Watch and pray. Then you won't fall into sin when you are tempted. The spirit is willing. But the body is weak."

³⁹Once more Jesus went away and prayed the same thing. ⁴⁰Then he came back. Again he found them sleeping. They couldn't keep their eyes open. They did not know what to say to him.

⁴¹Jesus returned the third time. He said to them, "Are you still sleeping and resting? Enough! The hour has come. Look! The Son of Man is about to be handed over to sinners. ⁴²Get up! Let us go! Here comes the one who is handing me over to them!"

Jesus Is Arrested

⁴³Just as Jesus was speaking, Judas appeared. He was one of the Twelve. A crowd was with him. They were carrying swords and clubs. The chief priests, the teachers of the law, and the elders had sent them.

⁴⁴Judas, who was going to hand Jesus over, had arranged a signal with them. "The one I kiss is the man," he said. "Arrest him and let the guards lead him away."

⁴⁵So Judas went to Jesus at once. He said, "Rabbi!" And he kissed him.

⁴⁶The men grabbed Jesus and arrested him.

⁴⁷Then one of those standing nearby pulled his sword out. He struck the servant of the high priest and cut off his ear.

⁴⁸"Am I leading a band of armed men against you?" asked Jesus. "Do you have to come out with swords and clubs to capture me? ⁴⁹Every day I was with you. I taught in the temple courts, and you didn't arrest me. But the Scriptures must come true."

⁵⁰Then everyone left him and ran away.

⁵¹A young man was following Jesus. The man was wearing nothing but a piece of linen cloth. When the crowd grabbed him, ⁵²he ran away naked. He left his clothes behind.

Jesus Is Taken to the Sanhedrin

⁵³The crowd took Jesus to the high priest. All the chief priests, the elders, and the teachers of the law came together.

⁵⁴Not too far away, Peter followed Jesus. He went right into the courtyard of the high priest. There he sat with the guards. He warmed himself at the fire.

⁵⁵The chief priests and the whole Sanhedrin were looking for something to use against Jesus. They wanted to put him to death. But they did not find any proof. ⁵⁶Many witnesses lied about him. But their stories did not agree.

⁵⁷Then some stood up. They gave false witness about him. ⁵⁸"We heard him say, 'I will destroy this temple made by human hands. In three days I will build another temple, not

made by human hands.' " ⁵⁹But what they said did not agree.

⁶⁰Then the high priest stood up in front of them. He asked Jesus, "Aren't you going to answer? What are these charges these men are bringing against you?"

⁶¹But Jesus remained silent. He gave no answer.

Again the high priest asked him, "Are you the Christ? Are you the Son of the Blessed One?"

⁶²"I am," said Jesus. "And you will see the Son of Man sitting at the right hand of the Mighty One. You will see the Son of Man coming on the clouds of heaven."

⁶³The high priest tore his clothes. "Why do we need any more witnesses?" he asked. ⁶⁴"You have heard him say a very evil thing against God. What do you think?"

They all found him guilty and said he must die.

⁶⁵Then some began to spit at him. They blindfolded him. They hit him with their fists. They said, "Prophesy!" And the guards took him and beat him.

Peter Says He Does Not Know Jesus

⁶⁶Peter was below in the courtyard. One of the high priest's women servants came by. ⁶⁷When she saw Peter warming himself, she looked closely at him.

"You also were with Jesus, that Nazarene," she said.

⁶⁸But Peter said he had not been with him. "I don't know or understand what you're talking about," he said. He went out to the entrance to the courtyard.

⁶⁹The woman servant saw him there. She said again to those standing around, "This fellow is one of them."

⁷⁰Again he said he was not.

After a little while, those standing nearby said to Peter, "You must be one of them. You are from Galilee."

⁷¹He began to call down curses on himself. He took an oath and said to them, "I don't know this man you're talking about!"

⁷²Just then the cock crowed the second time. Then Peter remembered what Jesus had spoken to him. "The cock will crow twice," he had said. "Before it does, you will say three times that you don't know me." Peter broke down and cried.

Jesus Is Brought to Pilate

15 It was very early in the morning. The chief priests, with the elders, the teachers of the law, and the whole Sanhedrin, made a decision. They tied Jesus up and led him away. Then they handed him over to Pilate.

²"Are you the king of the Jews?" asked Pilate.

"Yes. It is just as you say," Jesus replied.

³The chief priests brought many charges against him. ⁴So Pilate asked him again, "Aren't you going to answer? See how many things they charge you with."

⁵But Jesus still did not reply. Pilate was amazed.

⁶It was the usual practice at the Passover Feast to let one prisoner go free. The people could choose the one they wanted. ⁷A man named Barabbas was in prison. He was there with some other people who had fought against the country's rulers. They had committed murder while they were fighting against the rulers. ⁸The crowd came up and asked Pilate to do for them what he usually did.

⁹"Do you want me to let the king of the Jews go free?" asked Pilate. ¹⁰He knew that the chief priests had handed Jesus over to him because they were jealous. ¹¹But the chief priests stirred up the crowd. So the crowd asked Pilate to let Barabbas go free instead.

[12]"Then what should I do with the one you call the king of the Jews?" Pilate asked them.

[13]"Crucify him!" the crowd shouted.

[14]"Why? What wrong has he done?" asked Pilate.

But they shouted even louder, "Crucify him!"

[15]Pilate wanted to satisfy the crowd. So he let Barabbas go free. He ordered that Jesus be flogged. Then he handed him over to be nailed to a cross.

The Soldiers Make Fun of Jesus

[16]The soldiers led Jesus away into the palace. It was called the Praetorium. They called together the whole company of soldiers.

[17]The soldiers put a purple robe on Jesus. Then they twisted thorns together to make a crown. They placed it on his head. [18]They began to call out to him, "We honour you, king of the Jews!" [19]Again and again they hit him on the head with a stick. They spat on him. They fell on their knees and pretended to honour him.

[20]After they had made fun of him, they took off the purple robe. They put his own clothes back on him. Then they led him out to nail him to a cross.

Jesus Is Nailed to a Cross

[21]A man named Simon from Cyrene was passing by. He was the father of Alexander and Rufus. Simon was on his way in from the country. The soldiers forced him to carry the cross.

[22]They brought Jesus to the place called Golgotha. The word Golgotha means The Place of the Skull. [23]Then they gave him wine mixed with spices. But he did not take it.

[24]They nailed him to the cross. Then they divided up his clothes. They cast lots to see what each of them would get.

²⁵It was nine o'clock in the morning when they crucified him. ²⁶They wrote out the charge against him. It read, THE KING OF THE JEWS.

²⁷/²⁸They crucified two robbers with him. One was on his right and one was on his left.

²⁹Those who passed by shouted at Jesus and made fun of him. They shook their heads and said, "So you are going to destroy the temple and build it again in three days? ³⁰Then come down from the cross! Save yourself!"

³¹In the same way the chief priests and the teachers of the law made fun of him among themselves. "He saved others," they said. "But he can't save himself! ³²Let this Christ, this King of Israel, come down now from the cross! When we see that, we will believe."

Those who were being crucified with Jesus also made fun of him.

Jesus Dies

³³At noon, darkness covered the whole land. It lasted for three hours. ³⁴At three o'clock Jesus cried out in a loud voice, *"Eloi, Eloi, lama sabachthani?"* This means "My God, my God, why have you deserted me?" [PSALM 22:1]

³⁵Some of those standing nearby heard Jesus cry out. They said, "Listen! He's calling for Elijah!"

³⁶One of them ran and filled a sponge with wine vinegar. He put it on a stick. He offered it to Jesus to drink. "Leave him alone," he said. "Let's see if Elijah comes to take him down."

³⁷With a loud cry, Jesus took his last breath.

³⁸The temple curtain was torn in two from top to bottom.

³⁹A Roman commander was standing there in front of Jesus. He heard his cry and saw how Jesus died. Then he said, "This man was surely the Son of God!"

[40]Not very far away, some women were watching. Mary Magdalene was among them. Mary, the mother of the younger James and of Joses, was also there. So was Salome. [41]In Galilee these women had followed Jesus. They had taken care of his needs.

Many other women were also there. They had come up with him to Jerusalem.

Jesus Is Buried

[42]It was the day before the Sabbath. That day was called Preparation Day. As evening approached, [43]Joseph went boldly to Pilate and asked for Jesus' body. Joseph was from the town of Arimathea. He was a leading member of the Jewish Council. He was waiting for God's kingdom.

[44]Pilate was surprised to hear that Jesus was already dead. So he called for the Roman commander. He asked him if Jesus had already died. [45]The commander said it was true. So Pilate gave the body to Joseph.

[46]Then Joseph bought some linen cloth. He took the body down and wrapped it in the linen. He put it in a tomb cut out of rock. Then he rolled a stone against the entrance to the tomb.

[47]Mary Magdalene and Mary the mother of Joses saw where Jesus' body had been placed.

Jesus Rises From the Dead

16 The Sabbath day ended. Mary Magdalene, Mary the mother of James, and Salome bought spices. They were going to apply them to Jesus' body.

[2]Very early on the first day of the week, they were on their way to the tomb. It was just after sunrise. [3]They asked each other, "Who will roll the stone away from the entrance to the tomb?"

[4]Then they looked up and saw that the stone had been rolled away. The stone was very large.

[5]They entered the tomb. As they did, they saw a young man dressed in a white robe. He was sitting on the right side. They were alarmed.

[6]"Don't be alarmed," he said. "You are looking for Jesus the Nazarene, who was crucified. But he has risen! He is not here! See the place where they had put him. [7]Go! Tell his disciples and Peter, 'He is going ahead of you into Galilee. There you will see him. It will be just as he told you.'"

[8]The women were shaking and confused. They went out and ran away from the tomb. They said nothing to anyone, because they were afraid.

---

[9]Jesus rose from the dead early on the first day of the week. He appeared first to Mary Magdalene. He had driven seven demons out of her. [10]She went and told those who had been with him. She found them crying. They were very sad. [11]They heard that Jesus was alive and that she had seen him. But they did not believe it.

[12]After that, Jesus appeared in a different form to two of them. This happened while they were walking out in the country. [13]The two returned and told the others about it. But the others did not believe them either.

[14]Later Jesus appeared to the Eleven as they were eating. He spoke firmly to them because they had no faith. They would not believe those who had seen him after he rose from the dead.

[15]He said to them, "Go into all the world. Preach the good news to everyone. [16]Anyone who believes and is baptised will be saved. But anyone who does not believe will be punished.

[17]Here are the miraculous signs that those who believe will do. In my name they will drive out demons. They will speak in languages they had not known before. [18]They will pick up snakes with their hands. And when they drink deadly poison, it will not hurt them at all. They will place their hands on people who are ill. And the people will get well."

[19]When the Lord Jesus finished speaking to them, he was taken up into heaven. He sat down at the right hand of God.

[20]Then the disciples went out and preached everywhere. The Lord worked with them. And he backed up his word by the signs that went with it.

NEW INTERNATIONAL READER'S VERSION

The New International Reader's Version – published as the 'New Light Bible' – is a simplified, easy-to-read translation from the same team of translators who worked on the world's most popular modern English language Bible, the New International Version.

Using shorter sentences, easier words and simple grammar it is ideal for those seeking a Bible in down-to-earth language.

Hodder & Stoughton produce a number of complete Bibles in the New Light translation. They include:

Popular Bible, with introductions to every book by Steve Chalke

Study Bible, with introductory material plus textual side notes and end notes on every page

Mass Market Bible, produced in the format of a mass market paperback novel

Children's Bible, with full colour illustrations

For a complete catalogue listing all editions available in Hodder & Stoughton's NIV and NIrV range, please contact Hodder & Stoughton Religious Books, tel: 020 7873 6060, fax: 020 7873 6059, email: religious-sales@hodder.co.uk